CAREERS *in Your Community*™

CAREERS
in
SCHOOL SAFETY

Keith J. Olexa

Rosen
YA™
New York

Published in 2019 by The Rosen Publishing Group, Inc.
29 East 21st Street, New York, NY 10010

Library of Congress Cataloging-in-Publication Data

Names: Olexa, Keith, 1967– author.
Title: Careers in school safety / Keith J. Olexa.
Description: First edition. | New York : Rosen YA, 2019 | Series: Careers in Your Community | Audience: Grades 7–12. | Includes bibliographical references and index.
Identifiers: LCCN 2018012925| ISBN 9781499467284 (library bound) | ISBN 9781499467369 (pbk.)
Subjects: LCSH: School police—Juvenile literature. | Schools—Safety measures—Vocational guidance—Juvenile literature. | Schools—Security measures—Vocational guidance—Juvenile literature. | School violence—Prevention—Juvenile literature. | Vocational guidance.
Classification: LCC LB2866 .O44 2018 | DDC 371.7/82023—dc23
LC record available at https://lccn.loc.gov/2018012925

Manufactured in the United States of America

Contents

Introduction

Al has been coming to Sea Cliff High School for over ten years; he spends his whole day there, but he's not a teacher, nor is he a student. Al is the high school's resource officer (often called an SRO)—their capable, kind—and to some people, controversial—one-man police force. That's not just talk either—Al's a real cop. He took the SRO job to take it a little easy, but he's found himself busier than ever.

Each morning Al walks the school building and its premises, checking for vandalism, theft, or for unauthorized trespassers. As a police officer, he can make arrests if needed. It's not his favorite part of the job, but it's rarely required. After that, he monitors the morning crush of students (and has brief chats or shares jokes with several of them). Al confers with the principal on any issues of the day—rumors of potential fights or acts of bullying or other abuses. Al assists the principal however he can; good will helps keep him informed of any district-wide policies that might affect his work.

Al then begins his midday hall patrol. It's a popular misconception that school resource officers harass the students, but that's the furthest thing from Al's mind. He just talks to them. He asks about their weekend or their parents; he makes sure a basketball player (whose team he coaches) remembers practice after school. Al reminds all the kids that he's there to help them and always listens

intently when they confide in him. Al finds this part of his job especially challenging but most rewarding. Earning a student's trust is hard, and losing it is very easy. He has seen the viral videos of other school resource officers

From the rise in student drug use and social media dangers to active shooters and looming terror threats, school security has become an in-demand career.

overstepping their bounds. He never wants to be confused with one of them. Al works tirelessly to defuse each crisis calmly, relying on force only as a last resort. He's broken up his share of fights, but defusing tension with words over fists is a more satisfying conclusion. He teaches that lesson wherever he can.

Another vital part of his job is counseling. Like countless other security officers, Al enlightens the students on the dangers of joining a gang or posting revealing pictures online, why selling drugs will land you in jail, or how he'll do everything he can to save the kids in his care should danger darken his school's halls.

Al's story reflects the life of all SROs. Being a school resource officer is an empowering, dynamic, educational, and potentially dangerous profession. It's not for everyone, but if working in a school, helping kids, and challenging oneself on all levels appeals to you, then this is a good career option. None require a college degree, though most require (but also provide) additional training. The following chapters will explore the path to becoming a school resource officer and how to land the right job for you.

CHAPTER One

What Is a School Safety Officer?

Officers whose job it is to keep students safe are actually a pretty recent addition to schools. In the 1950s, a police officer was assigned to a school in Flint, Michigan, in order to help improve the relationship between students and the local police. The program was a success and spread to other schools for the next forty years. After the school shooting at Columbine High School in 1999, the calls for increased school security suddenly skyrocketed, and more schools began to employ security officers.

Today, many schools hire security officers to help keep students and faculty safe, in addition to a myriad of other tasks. Officers who handle security in schools are often referred to as school resource officers, school safety officers, school security officers, or simply security guards, depending on the type of training they receive and what their jobs entail. Let's take a closer look at the different types of school security roles.

A school resource officer is the most common type of school security officer. This school resource officer is shown here doing the most vital part of his job: educating students.

Types of School Safety Officer

Those who are interested in a school security role will want to understand the different types of positions that exist and what kind of training they'll need to find employment within the field of school security.

The school resource officer is the largest and most visible of this type of job. It also requires the most training. Type "school" and "security job" into a search engine and you'll almost always get "school resource officer" as a result. SROs are public sector employees, meaning that they're real police, sworn officers of the law who receive special training on how to perform their school duties. These police officers work for the police department but are assigned to work in a particular school. SRO duties and obligations do reflect their law enforcement background—they're authorized to carry and use weapons in school. However, they're trained to embrace mentorship, law education, and community service as key parts of their new job.

School security officers are not sworn law officers but are hired school employees who receive special training and certification to perform their duties. The work details can vary from state to state. SSOs are underrepresented when compared to SROs—finding job posts featuring them isn't easy. Pay and benefits can vary, but salaries tend to be lower for security officers than for SROs, but security officer training is less intense than the tough police training.

A security guard is hired through a security agency and not through the school itself. Depending on the school and the security agency, both training and responsibilities can range from lax to rigorous, though the guard's role and responsibilities would resemble those of a store security guard. It's the least common of the options for schools, as often more training is required to interact with students.

In the following sections, we'll use the term "school safety professional" when referring to all types of school security officers.

RESETTING HOPE: TALKING WITH OFFICER MAUNDY

Alabama school resource officer Garrett Maundy worked as a school resource officer for six years before landing his dream teaching job. He happily relates his SRO experiences in an interview with the author.

"It was [a job] I chose," he begins, revealing that desire fuels SRO success. "Someone who doesn't want to do the work, doesn't need to be there."

A twenty-five-year police veteran, Maundy explains why SRO work came so easy:

I always wanted to be a teacher. I [also] wanted to try something more low-key. I did and I immediately fell in love with it.

Being a mentor [was rewarding]. Out on the street, dealing with kids, the same as those in the school, it's usually a setting you've been called to [on the police radio]. It's always bad [a bad experience]. [School] is different; the students see you in a different light, in a more positive light.

There were challenges, too—big, small, grave, and trivial. Maundy shares a curious one: smartphones.

The bad thing about [kids and] social media with their snap chat ... it creates fights, drama; things escalate, and when a police dog shows up to search something, the kids knew about it before we get out of the car. The other side of that ... if there's a shooter, or a disaster—a tornado or something. Then the phones wind up helping us, keeping us informed, letting us know where they're at.

Some of these kids, the only reason they come to school is to eat. You see them at 7:30 AM, and you see you have this chance to reset them ... they have these terrible home lives they go back to at 3:30, but here you have this chance to reset them at 7:30 from the 3:30 they returned to the day before.

The History of School Safety

At the start of the twentieth century, sending children to school went from being a right to an obligation, and it became illegal *not* to be in school. This wasn't a universally popular idea right from the start—to both kids and often parents—so the truant officer's job was actually pretty difficult. Often mocked in old films and cartoons, the truant officer was a long-suffering, dour official who was often the subject of jokes. But the truant officer performed an important duty—getting kids back in the classroom. Truant officers used many techniques to perform their

Kids pledging to the flag were also pledged—though they probably didn't appreciate it—to go to school. The truancy officer would help them preserve that "pledge."

duties; they would often "arrest" delinquent students in order to return them to their school or their parents. But long before that, there were truant officers whose job it was to make sure that students were attending school as it became mandatory to do so.

Truant officers slowly slipped out of the collective consciousness over the decades, seemingly lost to time, though their role never diminished in importance. Yet despite this lack of attention, truant officers still exist today, although today they are referred to as attendance officers or truancy specialists. This task is also sometimes part of a school safety officer's job.

Following the success of the Flint, Michigan, program, a similar program was launched in Tucson, Arizona, in 1963 by Chief Bernard Garmire. This program was the first to use the title "school resource officer." Garmire would be responsible for several other successes and is a key player in the development of school police officers. Not all programs were successful though. One launched in Saginaw, Michigan, in 1966 met with less success, many believe because too few officers were spread over a large number of schools. But this would help later programs fix this type of error.

By the late 1960s, the job of the resource officer was being formalized. A number of programs and systems were introduced to help officers engage better with students, which eventually launched a specific training approach called triad, which we'll discuss in more detail in the following sections. First employed in Cincinnati, Ohio, this approach was touted as a big success.

In the years following, programs with increasingly ambitious goals were tested all over the country, in places ranging from the West Coast to Florida, and success built on success. The Miami program was initiated by Chief Garmire himself, who traveled from Arizona to oversee the trial run.

The 1970s saw an attitude change in this still loosely defined initiative: the goal of SROs became less about police engaging positively with students—through mentoring and educating as originally conceived—and more about simply preventing crime. But the principles of triad were never completely abandoned, and despite this shift, the program gained momentum, and schools everywhere in the United States slowly swelled with resource officers through the 1980s and right into the 1990s.

In 1991, the National Association of School Resource Officers (NASRO) was founded. Their mandate was to promote resource officers in schools throughout the country via advocacy as well as effective training. As of 2018, NASRO was school resource officer's most vocal and influential partner and resource.

Cops in Schools

From 1993 onward, several events occurred that would catapult school safety professionals into the heart of the school security question. In 1994, the Gun-Free Act was passed by Congress, introducing a severe zero-tolerance policy toward students found to be in possession of a firearm on any federally funded school grounds. The penalty was at minimum a one-year mandatory expulsion. This act did not deter violence in schools appreciably, but it did encourage schools to hire more SROs in order to intercept this problem that was so feared during that decade.

DRUG FREE

GUN FREE
SCHOOL ZONE
VIOLATORS WILL FACE SEVERE
FEDERAL, STATE AND LOCAL
CRIMINAL PENALTIES

The 1994 Gun-Free Act's uneven procedural process caused problems, though it bolstered the popularity of security officers.

The next event, which occurred toward the close of the 1990s, was the rise of school security officers in schools, thanks in large part to a $750 million grant program entitled Cops in School (established by the COPS branch of the US Department of Justice). This allowed for the funding of 6,500 additional officers.

The final, and most distressing, event was the tragic mass shooting on April 20, 1999, at Columbine High School in Columbine, Colorado, which left twelve students and one teacher dead and twenty-four injured. Mass school shootings would become an increasingly common trend throughout the United States in the early twenty-first century, and each attack would foster changes to make schools safer—changes that were sometimes controversial and often of mixed effectiveness. But one thing was true: the rate of school security hires only rose after that. And this dovetailed with the hires of school safety professionals as well—even jobs that didn't have security as part of their job began to shift.

Today as we continue to see violence in schools, school security remains an important, if controversial, issue.

CHAPTER Two

What School Safety Officers Do

Now that you understand why school safety officers exist, let's explore what they actually do and what your work expectations will be should you decide to pursue a career as a school safety officer.

The main role of a school safety officer is to help maintain safety within a school environment. This applies to the school resource officer, school safety officer, or anyone in the role of security guard within a school. This not only means taking action if violence is occurring, but working to avoid violence altogether. Many schools employ the use of metal detectors or other means of ensuring that no one enters the school carrying a gun or other dangerous instrument.

School resource officers not only work to help prevent violence but also have an expanded role that provides a support system for students. SROs often work with school guidance counselors to help improve student grades and attendance.

Security officers mix training with technology to keep students safe. School security has intensified greatly since the end of the twentieth century.

The Triad

School resource officers work under the triad (known fully as the triad of responsibility), a vital part of any effective school resource officer's training and work ethic. It comprises three aspects or sides of officer training that are deemed necessary in order for SROs to do their duty effectively. While any school safety officer program could implement a modified triad program at the discretion of the school or school district, this program was created specifically to train SROs.

The three sides of the triad highlight the three key roles all SROs are expected to operate in to perform

Physical confrontation isn't the cornerstone of a security officer's job. Safety and education take precedence—as does positively engaging with the students.

their duties: the role of counselor, educator, and law enforcer.

The law enforcer side comprises all the work police officers would normally do in performance of their duties: arrests, investigation, etc. This part of the job also covers knowing about crime trends and public safety issues. In this capacity, the SRO typically engages with other agencies when dealing with criminal issues involving students.

In issues related to the law and public and personal safety, the SRO engages students educationally. This involves giving presentations and lectures and otherwise making students aware of personal safety issues, gang and drug-related issues, and other potentially hazardous issues within the school.

The final side of the triad is counseling. This covers a number of informal job aspects, like simply acting as an ear for troubled students to acting as a liaison with possibly troubled communities.

Rewards and Challenges

Despite many similarities, the differences between being a school resource officer and a school security officer (or other type of school security professional) are significant in several ways.

The school security officer, as a direct employee of the district and school board, answers to only the school. Those worried or disdainful cops in school might naturally gravitate to the SSO role. School resource officers may perform many similar duties to SSOs, but they don't work directly for the school board. They're police officers.

The benefits of each position also differ. SRO work is more challenging to acquire as it involves completing a rigorous police training regimen before even being considered for the post. An officer who has walked a beat for many years might find an SRO position desirable and easier to land than a fresh-faced rookie. Conversely, an SSO position requires completion of a less arduous training program (depending on the state) and would be both easier to complete and faster. Some school districts might require additional training or prerequisites before hiring.

Other duties seem very similar; both will devote extra time outside of a normal school day for the student's benefit—and both do present certain risks. The question of use of force is a tough one and in the end is a matter of disposition. Carrying a firearm into a school is a charged topic.

Lastly, range of job information and resources vastly favor the SRO over the SSO. Even dedicated searches online for SSO topics will like deliver SROs results. In the end, choosing one way or another will involve some thorough searching.

SUPPORT FOR THE SRO

Mass school shootings have been on the rise since 2000, resulting in many parents, students, and school officials calling for heightened security in schools. People want to feel protected.

(continued on the next page)

(continued from the previous page)

According to a 2015 report from the National Center for Education Statistics, 43 percent of all US public schools—including 63 percent of middle schools and 64 percent of high schools—employed school resource officers during the 2013–2014 school year. More than forty-six thousand full-time and thirty-six thousand part-time officers were on duty during that time, and the numbers are expected to increase. Pay rates are competitive, with SROs earning up to $90,000 annually. School safety officers and security guards pay rates are comparable, and each generally makes less than the SRO. And because SROs are police officers, their benefits in terms of vacation and insurance are identical.

This profession also enjoys more comprehensive and more varied support, ranging from the government (via the COPS program) to numerous private organizations like the National Organization of School Resource Officers.

The SRO option is demanding, but the rewards in terms of job stability and pay mean these cops are tops.

Making a Career Choice

SROs are trained law officers who have chosen to apply a considerable array of skills to help protect the public and educate the students in their care. They quickly

Being an SRO means being a cop. Whether acting as a first responder at school crime scenes or preparing threat assessments to curtail those crimes—the law comes first.

dominated school security by the late 2010s—and make a good career choice for anyone interested.

As of 2016, according to the Bureau of Labor Statistics, SROs enjoyed job growth of about 1 percent. A 2015 report, the IES Public School Safety and Discipline report, reveals the extent SROs are being used. The IES report showed that 30 percent of schools employed at least one part- or full-time SRO the previous year. On average, according to the Bureau of Labor Statistics, police and sheriff's patrol officers earn between $34,230 and $98,510 annually, depending on experience and job assignment. Within schools, the average salary is around $50,000 for nonsupervisory officers. Salary and opportunity for jobs increases in metropolitan areas of the United States, especially along the East Coast and in California, Texas, Illinois, and Florida. And depending on location, an SRO can expect to enjoy work benefits commensurate with regional police types. Other sources, like the National Association of School Safety and Law Enforcement Officials (NASSLEO), suggest this job title is only expected to grow from 2018 to the foreseeable future.

Fantastic work, but not easy to get. Being an SRO means being a cop. It's not possible to become an SRO without completing difficult police officer training. And SRO work might be dynamic and rewarding, but it isn't a nine-to-five, working-for-the-weekend position. Thriving as an SRO, just like any successful student, means some extracurricular participation. Monitoring halls, doing drug checks in the lockers, and breaking up the occasional fight comes along with some serious mentoring and education responsibilities. School resource officers instruct students via training videos and education lectures in partnership with agencies like D.A.R.E. (Drug Abuse Resistance Education) or G.R.E.A.T. (Gang Resistance Education and Training), as well as giving talks on how to deal with cyberbullying or sexually inappropriate behaviors and actions, especially through technology. This often continues with after-school programs and informal projects, like coaching school games.

The school resource officer's work often continues out of the school, too: working overtime, being on call, and participating in weekend and after-school activities. This isn't an official policy everywhere, but community outreach is fast becoming an aspect of the job. SROs who allow themselves to be invited into the lives of their student's neighborhoods, who become familiar with families, and who devote themselves to understanding their students outside of the classrooms often claim they enjoy more trust and are better able to help students with problems. This kind of outreach also helps mitigate some community fears about the police—a key aspect of the program that began in the 1950s and continues through triad training and things like it.

Interestingly, the most publicly familiar side of the triad—the most coplike one—is the side least addressed by SROs in a given day. This aspect of the job involves confronting criminal activity, disorderly conduct and gang-related issues, and addressing assault complaints and sexual assault charges like any police officer. The officer can make any arrest or write tickets for infractions. SROs have the authority to remove, even by force, unauthorized or banned individuals from campus or school property. They can also take appropriate action to prevent conflicts from happening or escalating, using force if necessary. Being a police officer makes the SRO the on-call coordinator between the school and other law enforcement agencies (as well as civil agencies) when addressing an investigation involving a member of the school or when faced with some potential or realized danger.

This role as police officer is what many voice their greatest issues and concerns over—those who simply dislike the idea of police and education being so close together and those who will cite everything from justice studies to YouTube videos to assert that SROs are real or potential abusers of power or that they enable a system to shuttle disenfranchised students and minorities more rapidly into prisons.

SROs draw heavily from the triad's second side to counter this argument—through their role as mentors. This "soft" charm role doesn't suit all law enforcement types. It's a demanding part of the job and a commitment. Taking the

Fears of guns in school and power abuses are all controversial issues SROs face. Race relations is also an unfortunate concern, and one the police work hard to address.

time to get to know the students as individuals, share meals with them, let them tell their stories, and help those who need help isn't easy. Part of the mentoring involves teaching about the various dangers that plague kids in school: bullying and cyberbullying, drug use, sexual inappropriateness, as well as teaching non-violent conflict resolution, gang-related dangers, and practical dangers ranging from vehicular safety to how to best survive an attack by an active shooter. In this role, a school resource officer has the best chance of changing a student's mind regarding what an SRO is and what he or she can accomplish.

The third side of the triad is often cited as the most important side of the job: SROs as legal/school educator and liaison. Here they'll work to resolve problems at all levels and, when possible, through means other than the legal system. SROs contact with administrators, teachers, students, parents, mental health professionals, and community-based stakeholders facilitate this part of the work. Regarding the students themselves, the SRO can help guide the troubled boy or girl to a proper caregiver, if it's an internal issue, or to a school counsellor or external social worker.

CHAPTER Three

Training for a Job in School Security

All types of school security jobs require some form of training. This training is often difficult, but it is necessary. This makes school security jobs different from many other career paths. You have to be ready for anything, and you're often responsible for human lives, so training is the necessary starting place.

This is most true for a school resource officer career—training is intense because it's police officer training, which is both physically and mentally grueling. It's not a path for everyone, but for those who like to push their limits, it's ideal.

Police Training

Police training is almost like minicollege. A trainee will study those law enforcement classics—defensive tactics, nonlethal weapons, and firearm skills—possibly alongside the issue of the "use of force," which focuses not on how to use force but in what situations force may or may not be required.

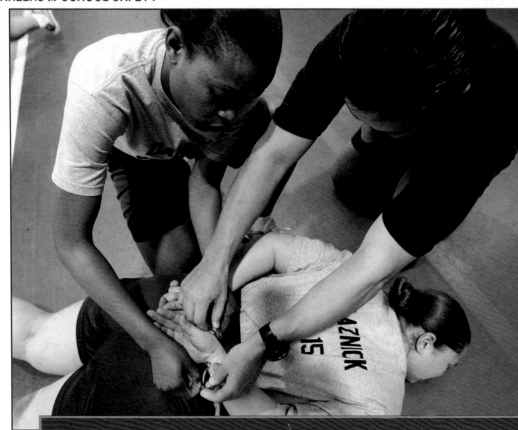

Taking a suspect down is part of a police officer's training—but this aggressive exercise will likely see a revision should one become an SRO.

Trainees will also study law: topics like legal knowledge, for example, a catchall for all the legal things police officers might do or notice in the line of duty. Another topic would be procedure, which are all the things a cop must do in the line of duty, like reading a suspect's rights during an arrest or handling an interrogation. Other topics might include fundamentals like apprehension and arrest or more advanced subjects like criminal psychology. And, of course, there are less popular but important subjects like report writing or database management.

Some topics might be surprising, like those related to public speaking and community outreach and collaboration. These are as important as self-defense and forensics in this very social media savvy world. Courses in civil rights laws and on improving one's appearance in public also exist.

And while the brain gets a workout, the body does, too. Physical fitness is essential. Most states have physical fitness standards required for academy graduates. In California, trainees must complete a timed run which involves navigating a long obstacle course, a 165-pound (75 kilogram) body drag, and man-height fence climbs before they can graduate. In Nebraska, according to a 2015 article on the Live Well Nebraska website, trainees must pass a fitness test before they are accepted into the program, including doing thirty-five sit-ups in a minute and completing a 1.5 mile (2.4 kilometer) run in thirteen minutes.

Trainee graduation requirements can differ depending on one's location in the country. The same basics exist everywhere, but particulars can vary state to state. Even similar graduation requirements can be subtly different.

Anyone who runs this gauntlet will be a cop, but to become a school resource officer requires more training. The good news? There's little to no physical training at this point. The bad news? Some police techniques that are useful and vital on the streets can be detrimental in the classroom. School resource officers should be prepared to learn some new things and also unlearn some things.

Engaging students in fun, creative activities can help a school security officer build trust. This trust gives students someone to confide in.

SRO's New Rules

At NASRO and other organizations like NASSLEO, one aspect of school resource officer training works to untrain some of an officer's previous skills. A potential clue exists in why some newly hired school resource officers resort to threats of arrest as a means of control mostly having to do with patterns of arrests that have occurred in response to minor infractions. NASRO and other groups see that improperly trained SROs can immediately view students as potential criminals, an issue heightened by their previous training. So courses like "Understanding the Teen Brain" and "Ethics and the SRO" can help a resource officer rethink potential problems in a more realistic manner.

Much of the SRO's training is inspired by the triad. Mentoring and education are two key aspects to the job, and counseling/liaising between police and the community is considered vital. A school resource officer is required to act as a teacher, to develop healthy mentor relationships with the students, and to be an active participant in school activities and extracurricular activities. This is an actual aspect of the job, which is reinforced by NASRO's supplemental training programs.

COMMON MISCONCEPTIONS OF THE SRO BRAIN

Although we often see or read about viral videos spreading that show school resource officers acting violently or inappropriately with students, it's a popular misconception that this is the norm. Here are some other misconceptions.

One misconception is that the job of a school resource officer is to maintain order in school. For many members of NASRO, like former resource officer Garrett Maundy, this is the opposite of the truth. Maintaining order in the school is up to the school administrator. Most school resource officers won't take physical action unless absolutely necessary. It's an extralegal discipline issue a number of SROs prefer to leave in school administrator's hands. Their involvement can turn any

(continued on the next page)

(continued from the previous page)

action into a criminal headache, especially where it will do the least good.

Another misconception is that school resource officers don't like students using smartphones in schools. The idea behind this is that students might film the officer committing a wrongdoing or using force in a situation where it isn't called for. But fearing a viral video isn't the cause for concern, Maundy explains, if the officer is doing his job well. And smartphones can be very useful during active shooter scenarios, where smartphones have been used to alert people outside of imminent danger and coordinate actions.

The last misconception is that any police officer can be a school resource officer. According to NASRO and other sources, hiring the right resource officer means finding the right temperament.

Training for a School Safety Officer

Compared to the training of an SRO, the training required for a school safety officer is far less demanding but still very important. A security officer is hired directly by the school and is therefore an employee like any other. There is no rigorous training like SROs face, but SSOs do have to complete a state or locally mandated security training course that would include many of the same kinds of topics covered in an SRO's training, though in a compacted form. Some school districts do allow a trained SSO to carry a firearm, but the job requires firearm training. Other skills, like first aid and cardiopulmonary

SROs receive ongoing firearms training to help keep students safe during an act of violence. Guns in the hands of anyone in schools, however, remains controversial.

resuscitation (CPR), might also be a requirement for hiring a prospective SSO. Training requirements vary from state to state, so if you're interested in this type of career be sure to research what the requirements are in your state.

The NYPD School Safety Officer course offers a helpful cross-section of the kinds of courses a school safety officer would take to become an SSO. They cover such things as school policing, dealing with special needs groups in a crisis, first aid, defensive tactics and physical fitness training, and dealing with terrorist threats in schools (which focuses on international terrorism in New York City but covers how to handle active shooter threats in schools). Though not cited above, any one of these topics might be used in training an SRO officer as well.

Security Guard Training

Security guard training is even less demanding. Often employees need nothing more than a clean record, a high school diploma, and eight hours of training before they can start working. Many states require security guards to be licensed before they begin working (often requiring guards to finish further training ranging by state from sixteen to forty hours upon deadlines that can range from weeks to several months away or else their provisional employment will be revoked). Some states, like Colorado and Mississippi, don't require any certification at all. And few require any physical training or tests, asking only that prospective hires be physically able to do the job. This can make a security guard job an attractive option—it's not as grueling as police training. Guard training does vary and much of it (like loss prevention) may not be suitable to schools. Beyond any federal state or local requirements, security companies might have requirements of their own specific to the agency.

Letters of Support

Training is key, but supporting organizations help also. They offer services, including more training, and they also help school security professionals do their jobs to the best of their abilities. Below is a small partners list, the meaning of their names, and how they help promote school security.

NASRO: National Association of School Resource Officers. They are the best partner that every SRO has and are an invaluable resource to anyone choosing SRO as a career path.

COPS: Community Oriented Policing Services, this branch of the U.S. Justice Department is devoted to promoting better policing in communities. This group is responsible for injecting $750 million into the SRO program in 1994.

D.A.R.E.: Drug Abuse Resistance Education. An organization started in 1983 by Los Angeles police officer Daryl Gates, created to curb drug use and gang recruitment. Despite very noble intentions, the organizations' programs by 2017 were repeatedly cited as being complete failures, both in the United Sates and the United Kingdom. No improved trend against drug use was ever shown. NASRO partnered with D.A.R.E., and one area where improvement was seen was in police community outreach, when D.A.R.E. officers trained with members of NASRO.

G.R.E.A.T.: Gang Resistance Education and Training. G.R.E.A.T. proved more successful than D.A.R.E. at accomplishing their goals. They also partnered with

NASRO, but investigation into their programs showed some positive outcomes, one of those being an increase in the number of parents and students who were more favorably disposed toward the police.

NASRO: The Best Resource for School Resource Officers

Many factors have come together to make school resource officers the most well-known part of the US school safety system, but NASRO is one of the most influential. Founded in 1991, The National Association of School Resource Officers (NASRO) has been a partner to SROs while also providing the highest quality of training to school-based

From NASRO to a school's administration, many groups interface with a security officer to help him do his job, be it in daily meetings or through improvement training.

law enforcement officers in the interesting of making both schools and children safer.

A global leader in school-based security, NASRO is a nonprofit organization that trains and supports school resource officers, and along with other school security and/or safety professionals, in conjunction with school administrators, partners with organizations dedicated to protecting faculty, staff, and most of all the students of our country's school system.

NASRO has been the strongest and most visible advocate for all SROs working in the United States since its inception. The triad system they developed has proven very effective in allowing SROs to interface with the students and perform their jobs more effectively. And with SROs now the fastest growing school policing force in the United States, NASRO can take satisfaction in being those officers' most visible partner. That distinction is not trivial; when a spate of videos went viral between 2015 and 2018 showing SROs exceeding their authority and use of force, NASRO saw the problem and pushed training that had been developed to help counter this behavior, along with the less obvious but more worrisome trend of targeting nonwhite students for incarceration.

For any who think SRO work sounds interesting, check out the NASRO website, or become a member. The training opportunities, services, and contacts make NASRO the SRO one-stop job shop.

The school resource officer job is more than just a job, though; it's a vocation that each officer spends many hours, days, and weekends enhancing and improving. It's an investment in the future, it's tough, and it's rewarding.

CHAPTER Four

Challenges on the Job and Other Career Options

The biggest downside of a career as a school safety officer is that the jobs are pretty scarce. Looking for postings for this type of job online can be frustrating, but the jobs are out there. They are often listed under different names like "school safety agent." Job openings are going to require different job requirements on a case-by-case basis, so be prepared to meet the requirements. Each job opening is going to feature different requirements and challenges.

According to the Bureau of Labor Statistics, the average SSO income ranged between $29,000 and $36,000 in 2016 (estimates, as SSO has no official distinction on file and a job's requirements can vary). An SSO is hired directly by the school or school district. They work for academia and are directly answerable to that body. Beyond that, SROs and SSOs will perform similar duties day to day. Sometimes the differences will be very

School resource officers, like Tiffany Wiggins, often patrol a number of schools within a district, interacting with students and staff in each location and working to build a good relationship with them.

minor seeming or specific. Both types of officer can detain students, though an SSO typically does this for the sake of the school administration itself, whereas an SRO does this because of a possible criminal activity.

Conversely, SROs can use force—even deadly force—in pursuit of their work. For an SSO, except in the most extreme circumstances, coercion of any kind is used against a student with great care and as a last resort. Both officers engage in mentoring and furthering education with the students. And where both coexist in a school district, an SSO will often partner with an SRO when addressing a school issue that might be especially dangerous. Potential active shooter activity or serious drug-related issues on school property fall under that category.

A quick look at any job site will show just how different one school security officer job can be from another, but a few common threads appear. All SSO jobs require only a high school diploma or GED education (though additional skill sets are often preferred and higher education never hurts) and expect a candidate to be modestly fit physically or at least able to perform reasonable physical tasks. Constant mention of criminal and background checks suggest prior convictions would disqualify one for the job. Beyond education and fitness, driver's licenses are preferred and typically required. Several job descriptions point out that while carrying a firearm is not a requirement, being trained in the use of firearms is a bonus. The job posts often cite that it's not a job for sitting down. Expect to be standing/walking a lot, inside or out and in any type of weather.

A few job listings expect a candidate be certified in CPR (and in some cases, the use of an AED—automated external [heart] defibrillator). This may look like a lot of extra things to have to know for this job, but it's not much different than with SROs, except that they gain many of those skills through their police training.

Security Guard

While it's possible to work as a security guard in any school, it's not common. Typical security guards aren't controlled by a school system (as SSOs are) or law enforcement (as SROs are). But the jobs exist, and if nothing else, working in security can certainly work in one's favor for landing a future SSO or SRO job.

Security guard job requirements and responsibilities vary state to state—many states require security guards to be licensed, which involves training that ranges from sixteen to forty or more hours, but in most cases, allow guards to work after eight hours. Some states, like Colorado and Mississippi, waive the licensing requirements, while Illinois requires licensing only for specific aspects of the job. Firearms in all cases are considered as a separate licensing issue, with armed guards requiring more intensive training than unarmed guards.

In a school, a security guard's job duties are very hands off. They don't mentor to kids or do much education work. Security guards will maintain order and deal with possible security issues in school, and that's it. Like SSOs, their ability to use force to control a student tends to be very sharply defined and limited. Their salaries are lower than those of other school security professionals, around $25,840 annually or at an hourly wage of around $12 to $13, the average of the last few years, though this can vary by experience and the company you work for. Unfortunately, many security guards who work for an hourly wage are not offered benefits, so keep an eye out for that during your job search.

If working for a school matters in any job hunt, then a security guard position may not be right. Guarding schools and/or students is not a common assignment for a typical security guard, and few groups can assure that work.

Challenges of the Job

There's another issue that have many favoring SSOs. Regular accusations are directed at SROs of racial profiling and speeding poorer and especially nonwhite students into the US prison system in a pattern known as

There are concerns that policing in schools creates a "pipeline" to jail for young people who commit serious or nonserious offenses.

the school-to-prison pipeline. This allegedly begins when a minor infraction—talking back, for example—is punished as if it were a crime (commonly under the term "disorderly conduct"). The student is rarely convicted, but the whole ordeal familiarizes the student to the process. The disruptive experience can adversely affect a student. Blacks and Hispanics, studies allege, are targeted more often in these exchanges. This issue is a lightning rod that charges those already unhappy with the overflow of police presence in public schools.

One reason an SSO position may be preferential to some over an SRO position is it doesn't carry any stigma that the SRO job can carry. SROs have been accused of criminalizing mere disruptive outbursts—all too common in any school—rather than taking an informal approach. The option is better and doesn't feed a narrative that SROs are contributing to the "school to pipeline" system of mass incarceration. Even modest legal stresses can severely disrupt students' lives, ultimately leading to dropping out, whereas dealing with a modest infraction without criminal prosecution can save students from a possibly devastating blow to their scholastic careers. SSOs face such challenges rarely, which some might find preferable.

Police organizations, spearheaded by NASRO, discussed the need for better SRO training. Seeing that the SRO position wasn't for everyone, officers began to be more thoroughly screened for the job—with a focus in selecting candidates who are best suited to deal with young people and react appropriately to difficult interactions with student stresses and the considerations of special needs kids. Some current indications point to apparent success, but there are people—both parents and concerned citizens—who still voice concerns over the police imposition in our school system and still believe, via concerns of racial profiling and the dangers of promoting juvenile incarceration, that a cop has no place in the classroom. One thing can't be argued, though: school security is indispensable, and that means job security is strong—and while the job has its challenges it also offers great rewards. But even as school safety professionals were becoming more commonplace in schools, cracks in their effectiveness began to be seen. During the late 2010s, a spate of viral videos appeared showing these officers using excessive force on students in videos revealing handcuffed and tasered children. This coincided with reports emerging that questioned the SRO's effectiveness and suggested possible dangers.

Other Types of Security

A school resource or safety career is a big commitment. There's training and a lot of risk involved. If working in school security is not for you, but you still want to explore some options that allow you to engage with students, maybe one of the following jobs is right for you.

School Crossing Guard

This is a time-honored and underappreciated position in any school system, but is it really a security job? The New York Police Department thinks so. It offers training to anyone who's interested in the position. The pay is lower than that of a school security professional—between $11 and $15 per hour—but the position can accrue benefits for an employee who works twenty-plus hours a week. It's part-time work—and slim at that—as a crossing guard is needed for two or so hours, twice a day, but it's ideal for certain kinds of workers: a person who works part-time elsewhere or someone who wants just a little extra income. It's a good starting job, too, as previous work experience is often not required, just a high school degree or equivalent.

If there's a downside, it's the hours themselves, which are scant, and that it's outdoor work in any kind of weather. Each state or city agency will offer training classes lasting several days that will always be accompanied by an extensive background check as the job involves working alone with children.

Beyond shepherding rowdy kids across busy intersections, crossing guards watch out for dangerous

Though school crossing guards are authorized to manage the roadway on a temporary, situational basis (stopping cars to help a fallen student), they cannot otherwise direct traffic.

and troublesome drivers or vehicles in the area, taking down license plates when possible; if a driver is a persistent menace, the police are contacted. A crossing guard is also responsible for reporting disruptive or unruly students to their teacher, parents, or other authority, but they're never to engage. A key consideration is a crossing guard is not trained to confront problems directly, only to report behavior back to someone who can better address the issue, like an SRO or the school's principal.

Truant Officer

If full-time work is preferred, but helping kids outside of school appeals (specifically if the interest is getting them back *into* school) then a job that many probably didn't realize still existed is an option: school truant officer (sometimes known as an attendance officer).

The job has changed a little since it first appeared to bring the school skippers back

49

to class. Attendance officers act as a sort of private investigator, tracking down missing persons—those students who skipped out on school. But now they can also be more like targeted guidance counselors, discussing the whys and hows of truancy and helping parents and others keep the kid in class.

Some students may consider absenteeism a joyride, but missing too much school can have dire consequences—not just to the student and not just in missed education. Penalties directed at parents or guardians can be severe. The degree to which school absences matter varies from state to state—some rules are comparatively lax, whereas in California chronic absenteeism can land parents or guardians in jail for a year and cost them $2,000 besides. Attendance officers also have the power to revoke the driver's licenses of chronically truant students.

According to the BLS, the 2016 median wage for attendance officers ranged between $60,000 and $70,000 annually. Like SSOs and SROs, an attendance officer's duties and responsibilities can vary from state to state and district to district. Like SROs, police can take on this role, but in other locations it operates more like social work or counseling and is open to anyone with training. There's some risk involved in this job. Truancy officers can find themselves in dangerous situations at times.

This job requires a high school diploma or GED, though more education helps. For those who don't wish to pursue that, the police route is best. If the counselor/social worker role appeals more, then some footwork may be needed. Finding a job fast might be challenging as many municipalities prefer (or even require) higher education for accreditation—though there are places in the United States that don't. Work hours for both sides of the profession tend to fall into the typical school day framework, since it's during school hours that students are going to skip school. There may be after-school work as well, as meeting with parents/guardians along with the students can help determine what issues may exist in the home, if any, and otherwise help parents to resolve this thorny problem.

OFFENSIVE DRIVING

The job of protecting students changes as history changes—it might once have been strange to see armed guards and metal detectors in high school, but after 9/11 people barely notice. Security extends beyond the classroom, too. Teachers and students both learn scary defense practices, and the danger has driven others to tighten their security training—literally in one case, as school bus drivers learn to be more secure. On January 29, 2013, in a quiet rural area in Midland, Alabama, a man killed a school bus driver and took a five-year-old boy hostage. After a tense, days-long stalemate, police eventually killed the kidnapper and saved the boy. Though this sounds like some unique

(continued on the next page)

(continued from the previous page)

spree killing story, it's not—it highlights the precariousness of school safety, where one must be vigilant even beyond the classroom.

School bus drivers all over the country began new training, embracing their new role as de facto security officers on wheels. The Connecticut School Transportation Association recently offered free security training to all drivers in the wake of global terrorist attacks. And the New Mexico Department of Transportation has developed an in-depth seventy-plus-page PowerPoint presentation that meticulously details what to do in the wake of kidnappers, active shooters, and terrorist extremists. That means more safety—for the driver and the student!

School Bus Driver

This job might seem like the most unlikely, and arguably the newest variation, but school bus drivers have actually been pulling school security officer duty, if informally, since the job appeared. They may have had the most dangerous security job of all: in the early twentieth century, children faced significant risk of injury and death just going to—and especially from—school. Before the school bus's ubiquitous yellow color and the strict no-passing rules became commonplace, children died often, struck by other drivers or the bus itself as

A school bus's lack of seat belts is, in fact, a safety feature! Tall, close-fitting seats make up for the belts, which might not release in an emergency.

they exited. While such disasters have become rare, school bus drivers still transport precious cargo to and from their school, ever aware that any accident would be a catastrophe.

That said, a high school diploma or GED is sufficient education for any school bus driver position (along with a CDL license and a background and criminal history check). The BLS lists the average salary at around $31,910 per year but, depending on skill and driving location, pay could go much higher.

CHAPTER Five

Landing the Job

Now that you know what a school security professional does, how do you go about getting a job as one?

To land a school resource officer position, the next step is inescapable. Join the police force. It's a hard step but essential to get the job. To secure a job as a

While cops with beards and long hair do exist (Sikh cops in New York City, for example, are now permitted to keep their long, faith-ordained hair), play it safe and shave.

school safety officer or other type of security professional, the process varies. But getting any position involves an interview. The advice below applies mostly to securing a police/SRO position, but many of these positions share similar dos and don'ts, so much of the advice presented can work for any security job hunt.

Dos and Don'ts of Your Security Job Search

To start, realize that some personal things can scuttle school security ambitions right away. Called automatic disqualifiers, these can vary depending by job or state, but if they crop up on a job application or during an interview, they'll stop the job hunt cold.

One of the most common and intractable of the disqualifiers is a felony conviction. Misdemeanors allow for some wiggle room, but they can slow the process. A physical or mental disability or condition that can't be effectively controlled and would impact the discharging of one's duty—severe hearing loss, uncontrolled seizure disorder, a debilitating heart or lung condition—all fall into this category.

Other disqualifiers are more subjective. Tattoos are a common one but not quite as disqualifying as they used to be. A bad credit history or a troubling background check (a history of domestic abuse, even without convictions) are both now less absolute job sinkers. Former drug use, and especially admitted drug addiction problems, can be a disqualifier. Background checks are common for these

Dress for success. Men should wear a suit, dress shirt, and tie to a job interview. Women should wear a suit, pants suit, or dress.

types of jobs, so be prepared and, most of all, *never lie* about any of these.

Discretionary things can affect employment chances. Any visible piercings beyond earrings for women, excessively long hair, and especially facial hair can disqualify a candidate. For both men and women, keeping hair neat, naturally colored, and of conservative length and style is just a safe bet.

This logic extends to clothing. There's no specific interview dress code that will secure that police job during the interview. Men should always dress in their best professional suit. Women should refrain from wearing anything revealing. Always dress professionally! In the end, always do homework regarding dress codes, liberality and such, but when in doubt, err on the side of a conservative appearance.

The Challenges of Police Training

A note regarding police officer training before going farther: getting into a police academy is no guarantee of success. Police training is incredibly hard. It's a combination of intense and grueling physical, intellectual, and, in some cases, psychological stresses that all occur within a relatively short time frame. Many don't make the cut because they're unable to keep up with the training, and given its physical demands, injury is often one reason that trainees are forced to drop out. This might sound promising if you succeed, but it means whoever is left is the best of the best. And in any environment where a profession is in demand, that will make competition high. Be prepared.

SAFETY DANCE

School security work isn't all about breaking up fights or dreading active shooters. Mentorship and education are equally if not more important. SROs and SSOs have responsibilities beyond safety. Perhaps because of the police stigma, SROs have gotten both creative and far-reaching in getting kids comfortable with them and in showing they're in school to help.

As Arkansas officer George Edelen puts it, "We don't want kids scared of us. We want them to feel comfortable coming to us whenever they need help or want to talk to us about something." Edelen is very popular with the students in King Elementary School, so for him to convince an entire student body of King Elementary to dance his "Wiggle Dance" with him in a video wasn't hard. Edelen did it to get the students excited about coming to school—the video going viral was a fun bonus.

Positive local community interactions vary as widely the schools they serve, and creative applications of this are being touted. SROs in a school district in Hollywood, Florida, for example, took the initiative by starting several community improvement programs including providing Thanksgiving meals for needy families, conducting a

(continued on the next page)

(continued from the previous page)

holiday toy drive, initiating Shop with a Cop, starting Story Time with an Officer, and beginning a Gang Resistance Education and Training (G.R.E.A.T.) program with their middle school students. Their work has been very successful.

SROs may not always have the easiest or most glamorous jobs, but when working in this capacity that build bonds, officers, students, and communities all want to dance to the same tune.

Policing the Interview Process

Starting with résumés and cover letters, consider some basics: keep the résumé conservative and chronological. Mention schooling, and always add special training (like CPR or firearms). Clean and informative is best. The same is also true of the cover letter. Highlight anything that might make an impression—educational experiences, etc.—and demonstrate an interest in where you're looking to be hired.

During the interview similar kinds of questions will arise—these relate to all types of security work. They're common because they're important. Answering them wrong can be a career killer.

Probably the most important set of questions any employer will ask will be related to self-control, temper, and when it's appropriate to use a weapon. They're important to any security position, so suggesting anger or loss of control when answering these questions, even as a joke, will kill that interview. When answering the

If asked a "how would you react if" question during an interview, a three-part answer that describes the situation, details the action taken, and highlights the results is best.

first two questions, describing past situations where hostilities were mitigated and tempers were calmed is good. Speaking very clearly and precisely about these moments is also good as it demonstrates self-control.

Regarding the weapon question, there is only one answer: speaking firmly and decisively, make it clear that weapons are to be used only in response to a life-threatening situation and only as a last resort. Even a sports hunting cop might raise an eye over a candidate too eager to have a gun in a school. Always go conservative.

And the last thing to remember: always do your homework before going into an interview. Learn as much as possible about the company or organization offering the job. If offered, ask questions. Show interest. That will go far in helping secure that security job!

From the Officer's Mouth

The following tips are pulled from several sources and relate to police/SRO jobs, but all can improve the chances of securing the kind of security position desired.

These first three tips, from too many sources to list, are essential musts for getting an edge up on the school security professional job hunt. First, stay physically fit. So, if you're not fit, get fit. All variations of these security jobs have that in common: they require some degree of physicality—so hit that treadmill. Second, demonstrate civic spirit. The easiest way to do that is volunteer, at a homeless shelter, food bank, or charity event. It goes a long way. And third, ask questions when prompted, basing them on due diligence. Ask specific things about

THE GUARDING AGAINST FAILURE CHECKLIST

Remember these eight things to make landing that ideal school job easy.

1. Think: Are there any auto-disqualifiers in my past? No? Go to number two. Yes? Find other work.

2. *Never* lie about anything during an interview. It's not smart, and it could be illegal.

4. Do your homework. This can't be overstated. Know the place you want to work in, the school, the district, everything. It shows you're interested.

5. Like kids. No avoiding it; this will be your day-to-day.

6. Be engaging. Few if any of these jobs are for wallflowers.

7. Dress well and look well. Short hair, clean shave, conservative everything else. It may be dull, but it's safe, and that will not hurt.

8. Speak clearly and decisively. The job needs strength, so demonstrate that from the start.

the company that's hiring. It shows thoughtfulness and interest.

From law enforcement career expert Sergeant Betsy Brantner Smith comes this funny insta-fail "advice" via

High-five for the safety officer! To land and keep that SRO or SSO job, one piece of advice is most important: be good to the kids and engage with them.

policelink.monster.com: "Make sure your social network sites show what a fun-loving party animal you really are." Smith's point: keep your visible life scrupulously clean. When you begin to look for work, any prospective employer will begin to scrutinize your social media presence. If it reveals an out of control wild child or suggests anything too strange or inappropriate or, worse, shows—or even suggests—any dishonesty or criminality, then kiss that job goodbye.

But perhaps the best bit of advice comes from Officer Garrett Maundy, addressing traits vital to succeeding as a school resource officer, but it's advice that works everywhere. "You've got to be personable," he says simply. And this goes beyond just being friendly, it also means being empathetic and listening before you act. There's a lot of power wrapped up in working in security. A little humanity goes a long way toward building trust and creating a positive, caring environment.

Glossary

ACTIVE SHOOTER A somewhat controversial term used by the Department of Homeland Security and other agencies to describe serial or spree killers known for the scale, suddenness, and randomness of their attacks, as well as by their often-suicidal tendencies.

ATTENDANCE OFFICER Also known, informally, as truancy officers, they work either as police or counselors to promote attendance in school and address issues related to unexcused school absences.

CIS Short for "COPS in School," a grant program awarded by COPS specifically to fund the placement of more police in the country's school system.

COPS Community Oriented Policing Service, a US Department of Justice program created to advance the practice of local policing throughout the country.

D.A.R.E. An acronym for Drug Abuse Resistance Education. A US safety organization founded in 1983 to combat rampant drug addiction and mounting gang activity.

GED General Equivalency Development or General Equivalency Diploma. A test-determined certification that is the equivalent of a United States or Canadian high school diploma.

G.R.E.A.T. Gang Resistance Education and Training. An organization founded in 1992 to combat the rising gang membership within the country through the teaching of life skills.

MENTORING Training or teaching of a younger or less experienced person in a specific way by an older or more experienced person

PRIVATE SECTOR The larger part of the national economy that is not under direct government control; this includes all businesses and any other forms of free enterprise.

PUBLIC SECTOR The part of the national economy that is under direct national control.

SCHOOL-TO-PRISON PIPELINE Referring to conditions believed by some to exist in post 9/11 school systems that are thought to send students (often nonwhites of poor socioeconomic background) to the prison system.

SCHOOL RESOURCE OFFICER (SRO) A sworn police officer, specially trained and assigned to provide security to schools or within a school district and also act as educators and law counselors.

SCHOOL SECURITY OFFICER (SSO) An academic alternative to SROs, SSOs are hired directly by the school they work in, operating primarily as school security officers as well as counselors and educators.

SECURITY GUARD This covers a number of security professions not expressly defined elsewhere but commonly refers to those who work for private sector companies to protect items, people, or locations.

SPECIAL NEEDS CHILD An umbrella term applied to children coping with a mild to severe physical or mental illness or disability, who often receive aid to help deal with their condition.

TRIAD The three-sided cornerstone of SRO training that combines traditional law enforcement practices with education and student mentoring as well as counseling/liaising duties within the community.

TRUANCY OFFICER An older, less commonly used named for attendance officer.

For More Information

Canadian Safe Schools Network
4229 Niagara Street
Toronto, ON M6J 2L5
Canada
(416) 977-1050
Website: http://www.canadiansafeschools.com
Facebook: @canadiansafeschoolsnetwork
Twitter: @CndnSafeSchools
A not-for-profit charity organization located in Ontario,
    Canada, Safe Schools is dedicated to eliminating
    youth-related acts of violence in the effort to make
    schools and communities safer.

Gang Resistance Education and Training (G.R.E.A.T.)
PO Box 12729
Tallahassee, FL 32317-2729
(800) 726-7070
Website: http://www.great-online.org
Facebook: @GREATprogram
Founded in 1992, G.R.E.A.T. is dedicated to reducing the
    prevalence of gangs and gang violence throughout
    the United States by using effective evidence-based
    methods and tools to empower young boys and girl to
    make healthier life choices.

International Foundation for Protection Officers
1076 6th Avenue, North
Naples, FL. 34102
(239) 430-0534
Website: http://www.ifpo.org
Facebook: @ifpo.org
Twitter: @ifpoNEWS

An international organization dedicated to providing highly comprehensive services related to all forms of security work all over the world. They're very comprehensive, offering training, news, and networking; their data base and journal entries seem expansive, but they do offer a modest focus on school security and do seem to provide some information on work opportunities for security guards.

National Association of School Resource Officers (NASRO)
2020 Valleydale Road, Suite 207A
Hoover, AL 35244
(888) 316-2776
Website: http://www.nasro.org
Facebook: @nasro.org
Twitter: @nasro_info
The National Association of School Resource Officers (NASRO) is the largest not-for-profit advocacy and training organization created to support the placement of school resource officers in schools around the country and to provide services and training as needed.

National Association of School Safety and Law-Enforcement Officials (NASSLEO)
3800 NW 27th Avenue
Miami, FL 33142
(760) 472-3389
Website: http://www.nassleo.org
Facebook: @NASSLEO
Instagram: @NASSLEO1
The National Association of School Safety and Law-Enforcement Officials (NASSLEO) is an organization

dedicated to uniting all types of security professionals with school officials to promote and build a safe school system. It is reminiscent of NASRO with similar but more expansive goals dedicated to all members of the school security community. NASSLEO is also more decentralized, operating in seven regions around the United States.

National Association of Security Companies (NASCO)
NASCO National Headquarters
444 North Capitol Street NW, Suite 203
Washington, DC 20001
(202) 347-3257
Email: information@nasco.org
Website: http://www.nasco.org
The National Association of Security Companies (NASCO) was founded to support all security guard professions in the private sector. It offers a number of good resources and is the ideal organization to join if working as a school security guard appeals.

National School Safety Center
141 Duesenberg Drive, Suite 7B
Westlake Village, California 91362
(805) 373-997
Website: http://www.schoolsafety.us
The National School Safety Center is an advocate for peaceful schools worldwide. They promote all aspects of school safety. They focus on preparedness and personal preparedness.

Toronto District School Board
5050 Yonge Street
North York, ON M2N 5N8
Canada
(416) 397-3000
Website: http://www.tdsb.on.ca
Facebook: @Toronto.dsb
Twitter: @tdsb
Instagram: @Torontodsb
This is the largest school board in Canada and one of
the most culturally diverse. In summer 2017, the
board approved a plan to review the use of school
resource officers in a selection of its 584 schools.
This is one of the best resources to learn about SRO
programs in Canada.

US Bureau of Labor Statistics
Postal Square Building, 2 Massachusetts Avenue NE
Washington, DC 20212-0001
(202) 691-5200
Website: http://www.bls.gov
A part of the US Department of Labor, the BLS is an
excellent resource to learn about working trends and job
statistics throughout the country. Database data follows
employment by profession, region, and other criteria.

For Further Reading

Brenig, Hidley. *Investigating Mass Shootings in the United States.* New York, NY: Rosen Publishing, 2018.

Brezina, Corona. *Alcohol and Drug Offenses: Know Your Rights.* New York, NY: Rosen Publishing, 2015.

Freedman, Jeri. *Careers in Security.* New York, NY: Rosen Publishing, 2014.

Gill, Floyd *W. Badge on Campus.* New York, NY: Advanced Publishing, 2016.

Harmon, Daniel E. *Working as a Law Enforcement Officer in Your Community* (Careers in Your Community). New York, NY: Rosen Publishing, 2015.

Johnston, Coy. *Careers in Law Enforcement.* Los Angeles, CA: SAGE, 2016.

May, David C. *School Safety in the United States: A Reasoned Look at the Rhetoric.* Durham, NC: Carolina Academic Press, 2014.

Nijkamp, Marieke. *This is Where It Ends.* New York, NY: Sourcebooks Fire, 2016.

Puckett, James. *The School Security Officer: What Makes a Good One?* New York, NY: Archway Publishing, 2014.

Smith, Marilyn, Matthew Monteverde, and Henrietta Lily. *School Violence and Conflict Resolution.* New York, NY: Rosen Publishing, 2013.

Wolny, Philip. *Defeating Gangs in Your Neighborhood and Online.* New York, NY: Rosen Publishing, 2015.

Bibliography

Alphonso, Caroline. "Students Benefit from Police in Schools, Study Suggests." *Globe and Mail*, January 10, 2018. https://www.theglobeandmail.com/news /toronto/students-benefit-from-police-in-schools -study-suggests/article37569442.

Canady, Maurice, Bernard James, and Janet Nease. "To Protect and Educate." NASRO15, 2012. https://nasro .org/cms/wp-content/uploads/2013/11/NASRO-To -Protect-and-Educate-nosecurity.pdf.

Childress, Sarah. "Do Cops in Schools Know How to Police Kids?" *Frontline*, May 4, 2016. https://www.pbs .org/wgbh/frontline/article/do-cops-in-schools-know -how-to-police-kids.

Esbensen, Finn-Aage. "Evaluation of the Gang Resistance Education and Training (G.R.E.A.T.) Program in the United States, 1995–1999." Inter-university Consortium for Political and Social Research, August 21, 2018. https://library.carleton.ca/sites/default/files/find/data /surveys/pdf_files/egreat-us-95-99-gid.pdf.

Finn, P. M. Townsend, M. Shively, and T. Rich "A Guide to Developing, Maintaining, and Succeeding with Your School Resource Officer Program." Department of Justice, Office of Community Oriented Policing Services, February 16, 2016. http://www.popcenter.org /Responses/school_police/PDFs/Finn_et_al_2005.pdf.

Gray, Lucinda, Laurie Lewis, and John Ralph. "Public School Safety and Discipline: 2013–14." First Look, May 21, 2015. https://nces.ed.gov/pubsearch/pubsinfo .asp?pubid=2015051.

Hammel, Paul. "Nebraska Police Academy's New Fitness Standards Draw Criticism from Smaller, Recruit-Hungry

Agencies." Live Well Nebraska, December 22, 2015. http://www.omaha.com/livewellnebraska/fitness /nebraska-police-academy-s-new-fitness-standards -draw-criticism-from/article_c74b3cf6-4233-59c0 -97b2-4544b5da4f79.html.

Kiernan Coon, Julie, and Lawrence Travis III. "The Role of Police in Public Schools: A Comparison of Principal and Police Reports of Activities in Schools." Police Practice and Research, October 13, 2011. https://www.tandfonline .com/doi/abs/10.1080/15614263.2011.589570.

Lynch, Caitlin Grace. "School Resource Officers and the School-to-Prison Pipeline: A Mixed Methods Application of the Behavior of Law in Schools." Sociology and Criminal Justice Theses & Dissertations, Summer 2017. https://digitalcommons.odu.edu /cgi/viewcontent.cgi?referer=https://www.google .com/&httpsredir=1&article=1013&context=sociology _criminaljustice_etds.

Maundy, Garrett. Phone interview with the author, February 15, 2018.

Na, Chongmin, and Denise Gottfredson. "Police Officers in School: Effects on School Crime and the Processing of Offending Behaviors." *Justice Quarterly*, October 3, 2011. https://ccjs.umd.edu/sites/ccjs.umd.edu/files/pubs /Police%20Officers%20in%20Schools-Effects%20 on%20School%20Crime%20and%20the%20 Processing%20of%20Offending%20Behaviors.pdf.

Nathan, James "Analyst in Crime Policy Gail McCallion Specialist in Social Policy School Resource Officers." Law Enforcement Officers in Schools, June 26, 2013. https://fas.org/sgp/crs/misc/R43126.pdf.

National Association of School Resource Officers. "Frequently Asked Questions—National Association of School Resource Officers." Retrieved February 12, 2018. https://nasro.org/frequently-asked-questions.

Nordrum, Amy. "The New D.A.R.E. Program—This One Works." *Scientific American*, September 10, 2014. https://www.scientificamerican.com/article/the-new-d-a-r-e-program-this-one-works.

Robinson, Teresa Renee. "Understanding the Role of the School Resource Officer (SRO): Perceptions from Middle School Administrators and SROs." University of Tennessee, December 2006. http://trace.tennessee.edu/utk_graddiss/2027.

Smith, Betsy Brantner. "Ten Common Ways to NOT Get Hired." PoliceLink. Retrieved February 8, 2018. http://policelink.monster.com/benefits/articles/87180-ten-common-ways-to-not-get-hired.

Thomas, Benjamin, Laura Towvim, John Rosiak, and Kellie Anderson. "School Resource Officers: Steps to Effective School-Based Law Enforcement." NASRO, September 2013. https://nasro.org/basic-sro-course.

Vaught, Debbie. "School Resource Officers Make a Difference." *Herald and News*, March 31, 2012. https://www.heraldandnews.com/members/forum/guest_commentary/school-resource-officers-make-a-difference.

Wald, Joanna, and Lisa Thurau. "First, Do No Harm: How Educators and Police Can Work Together More Effectively to Preserve School Safety and Protect Vulnerable Students." Charles Hamilton Institute for Racial Justice, May 3, 2010. http://www.modelsforchange.net/publications/261.

Index

About the Author

Olexa began his career writing for entertainment periodicals before directing his energies to science and history articles and books. He has written on the histories of such things as the American militia, the rise of sea planes and the medal of honor, and covered science topics ranging from exoplanet astrophysics to the effects of the Paleolithic diet. Besides writing, Olexa edits for a number of publishing houses and authors. He has edited for reprint the works of the late Alan Drury, as well as books by Kevin J. Anderson, Mercedes Lackey, and Peter Wacks, as well as several anthologies. He has written his first book, *The Gross Science of Lice and Other Parasites*, for Rosen Publishing.

Photo Credits

Design and Layout: Nicole Russo-Duca; Editor: Bethany Bryan; Photo Researcher: Sherri Jackson